Growing Garden
Bulbs

RICHARD WILFORD

Contents

Introduction   **3**

Buying bulbs   **4**

Planting and caring   **6**
- Planting depths   **7**
- Naturalising bulbs   **8**
- Planting in grass   **8**
- Growing bulbs in pots   **10**
- Long-term care   **12**
- Pests and diseases   **13**
- Propagation   **14**

Bulbs by season   **16**

Winter
- Snowdrops   **18**
- Crocus   **22**
- Winter aconite   **24**
- *Cyclamen coum*   **25**
- Reticulata irises   **26**

Spring
- Daffodils   **28**
- Tulips   **32**
- Hyacinths and bluebells   **35**
- Fritillaries   **36**
- Small blue bulbs   **38**
- Dog's tooth violets   **40**
- Anemones   **41**

Summer
- Alliums   **42**
- Lilies   **44**
- *Camassia*   **47**
- *Gladiolus*   **48**
- Dahlias and begonias   **49**

Autumn
- *Colchicum*   **50**
- Autumn-flowering crocus   **52**
- Autumn-flowering *Cyclamen*   **54**
- *Sternbergia*   **57**
- Nerines   **58**

South African bulbs   **59**

Glossary   **60**

Introduction

Every garden, however large or small, should have some bulbs. Whether you have a simple window box or a vast country estate, bulbs can be planted to provide colour and drama. They can be part of a bold design scheme, a naturalistic meadow planting, a colourful border or a display of pots on a terrace. The appearance of a golden yellow daffodil catching the light of the morning sun is a sign that winter is finally loosening its grip, but bulbs aren't restricted to spring. They can flower at any time of year, from the depths of winter to the height of summer. The bulbs in this book are arranged by flowering season, providing a choice of plants that will ensure you can enjoy beautiful blooms all year round.

Daffodils are among the most commonly grown garden bulbs, with a bewildering range of varieties to choose from, but hot on their heels in the popularity stakes are tulips, lilies, snowdrops and crocus. There are the delicate winter irises, the waving summer drumsticks of alliums, wide goblets of autumnal colchicums, dazzling blues of grape hyacinths, squills and the evocative bluebell, and that is not all. The range of garden bulbs can be overwhelming, so be prepared to make some difficult choices, unless, of course, you do have that country estate, in which case you will have room to grow them all!

Richard Wilford

***Crocus tommasinianus* growing through the common snowdrop (*Galanthus nivalis*) in late winter** ▶

Buying bulbs

The word bulb is commonly used for a number of different types of plant, including corms and tubers, but they have one thing in common; they have a dormant dry period, usually in summer. Most are found naturally in regions that have a dry season, such as around the Mediterranean Sea, where they retreat underground to survive the summer drought. This makes them very easy to transport when dormant: most bulbs are sold in late summer and autumn when they have had their summer rest and are ready to grow as soon as they get some water. The range of bulbs that are dormant in the winter is smaller, but includes lilies, dahlias and begonias. These are sold in winter and early spring.

▲ **Packets of bulbs for sale in late summer**

The easiest way to buy bulbs is to head down to your local garden centre, nursery or supermarket, where bulbs will be displayed on shelves or racks, their packets illustrated with enticing photographs. If you can't find what you want there, try online. There are many bulb suppliers on the internet and their web pages are full of bulbs available to order. Online suppliers will generally have a wider range of varieties to choose from and include some bulbs that might be difficult to find elsewhere. If there is something in particular you are after, make sure to get your order in quickly, as the less common varieties will often sell out.

If you are buying your bulbs from a shop you can check them before you pay. Look out for plump, firm bulbs. Avoid those that are very soft, have rotten patches or have mould on the surface. The earlier you buy them, the healthier they are likely to be. You can get some great cut-price

▲ **Healthy bulbs of *Narcissus* 'Minnow' sold loose**

▲ **Bulbs to avoid, dehydrated and with mould growing on the surface**

4

bargains late in the bulb-buying season, but bulbs often suffer from sitting on the shelves for weeks or months as they can dry out too much. Some bulbs, like tulips and alliums, can withstand this treatment better than others. Also, look out for bulbs that have started growing while still in their packets. They will need planting straight away. This is especially true of the autumn-flowering colchicums, which can flower in the garden in early autumn and might try to do so while still in the shop. This won't kill them, but the flowers won't last long and you will have to wait another year to really enjoy them. Again, buying early is the best advice.

Of course, there is no point buying your bulbs early if you then leave them lying around for a month or more before planting them. If you can't plant straight away, keep the bulbs somewhere cool and dark until you are ready. It is best to plant them as soon as possible; they will be a lot happier in the ground.

You don't have to buy bulbs when they are dormant. Flowering bulbs can be bought in pots for an instant display. Shows, such as those run by the Royal Horticultural Society (RHS), are good places to buy growing bulbs and to find the more unusual varieties. Once the plants have finished flowering, make sure

▲ **Colchicum flowering in the shop before they have been sold — they will survive if planted immediately but the flowers won't last long this year**

▲ **A multitude of snowdrop varieties for sale at an RHS spring show**

that you plant them out in the garden, where they should flower again the following year. This is not always the cheapest way to buy bulbs, but it does mean they haven't been allowed to dry out in packets for too long. Buying snowdrops 'in the green' (after flowering but still in leaf) is fairly common practice now — you can purchase trays of newly dug up bulbs ready for immediate planting in your garden.

Planting and caring

Tulips grown as spectacular bedding plants, at the Cambo Estate garden, Scotland

Where and how you plant your bulbs will depend on the effect you are trying to create. In a formal bedding display, you may want to plant the bulbs in lines or shapes, forming squares or circles. Single varieties planted in a block make a bold display and tulips are ideal for this, with their large flowers and bright colours. Hyacinths and larger daffodils (*Narcissus*) are also great for bedding but also think about under planting them with smaller bulbs that flower at the same time, such as anemones or grape hyacinths (*Muscari*). The bulbs can be planted close together when used as bedding, as they are normally lifted once finished and relocated to less formal parts of the garden.

Narcissus 'February Gold' under-planted with blue *Anemone blanda*

Gladiolus byzantinus in a gravel garden

▲ **Planting tulips in a mixed border using a trowel to dig a hole for each bulb**

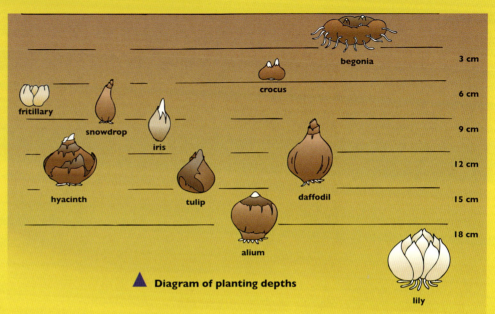

▲ **Diagram of planting depths**

In a less formal setting, bulbs can create a drift through a mixed border, planted in clusters or large groups and peering between shrubs or herbaceous perennials that will grow up and fill the space after the bulbs have finished flowering. Drifts of snowdrops, crocus, winter aconite (*Eranthis*) and varieties of *Iris reticulata* brighten up a border in late winter. For summer-flowering bulbs, you will need to consider how much the surrounding plants will grow between planting time, in winter or spring, and the height of summer, when the bulbs come into flower. Lilies can be grown in the dappled shade of a woodland garden and can be taller than the surrounding plants, which will form a green backdrop to the gorgeous blooms. Gladioli and alliums can be planted in a sunny border, with ornamental grasses or lavender and geraniums, for example.

Planting depths

A good general rule is to plant bulbs at a depth 3 times the height of the bulb. So for a bulb that is 2 cm tall, you should dig a hole 8 cm deep, which will leave 6 cm of soil above the bulb. Most bulbs can be planted deeper; *Iris reticulata* and tulips often prefer deeper planting. A few bulbs, including begonias and cyclamen, do better very near the soil surface. Place the bulbs on the ground in the locations where you want to plant them. Then dig a hole for each bulb with a trowel and plant the bulb, covering with soil and firming lightly. Leave space between each bulb to allow room for growth; about 10 cm between small bulbs and 30 cm for larger bulbs. Work from the back of a border to the front, so you end up on the path or lawn and don't have to walk back over ground in which bulbs are planted.

To plant a large number of smaller bulbs, you can use a spade to scrape away the soil and place the bulbs in a drift before putting the soil back to cover them. This is not so easy if you are placing them among other plants that you don't want to disturb, in which case, planting individually with a trowel is the better option.

Naturalising bulbs

Bulbs scattered randomly through a border or meadow, or pushing through a lawn, can give the impression that they are growing naturally and have not been planted. Different varieties can be mixed together or a group of one type can join and overlap with other groups to enhance the natural look. Over the years, the bulbs will increase in number, by producing seed that sows itself or by the bulbs themselves dividing underground to form a colony of plants that looks like a naturally occurring population. To achieve this effect, it is important to plant bulbs in a random pattern, with small clusters separated by gaps with few or no bulbs at all. This can be done by placing the bulbs individually, but all too often this results in a less than random pattern. It is usually more successful to stand up and throw a handful of bulbs onto the ground and plant them where they fall.

A few types of bulb, including cyclamen and the beautiful *Tulipa sprengeri*, can be naturalised in the garden by sowing their seed direct. Scatter the seed in a border in autumn and gently rake it in so that the seeds are covered. Seedlings will appear the following spring and two or three years later the first plants will flower.

A self-seeding colony of *Tulipa sprengeri*

▲ **Mixed daffodils growing in grass**

Planting in grass

Naturalised bulbs look most effective when growing in grass. Winter- and spring-flowering bulbs, such as snowdrops, winter aconite, crocus, snake's head fritillary and daffodils, are the best for naturalising in grass. When choosing a location, remember that the leaves of the bulbs should be allowed to die down before the grass is cut. The grass can grow quite tall before you can get the lawn mower out, especially where later-flowering varieties have been planted. Autumn-flowering crocus and *Cyclamen hederifolium* can also be grown in grass but once the flowers appear, grass cutting for that year must stop; the flowers are followed by leaves that remain all through the following winter and spring.

Crocus naturalised in a lawn ▶

Bulbs in grass need to be planted under the turf. For smaller bulbs, like crocus and snowdrops, a piece of lawn can be lifted to expose the soil and the bulbs placed on the ground before replacing the turf over them. If you cut a square of turf, don't fill the whole square to the corners with bulbs. Try to create a more random pattern; otherwise you will end up with a neat square of flowers the following spring.

For larger bulbs, such as daffodils, it is better to dig individual holes to ensure that the bulbs are planted deep enough. Throw the bulbs onto the ground to get that random pattern and use a trowel to dig a plug of turf where each one lands. Place the bulb in the hole and replace the turf plug over the top, firming it down to leave a level surface.

▶ **Planting daffodil bulbs individually in turf with a trowel**

▼ **Planting crocus corms under a square of turf**

1

2

3

▲ **Hand-held bulb planter**

▶ **Long-handled bulb planter**

A bulb planter can be used to plant in turf. These are either hand-held tools or have a long handle and foot-rest to allow the planter to be pushed into the ground by standing on it. The planter will cut out a plug of turf. Making the next hole will push the first turf plug out of the planter and this can be replaced over the first bulb. It is worth spending a little more to buy a well-made bulb planter, especially if you have a lot of bulbs to plant. In hard or stony ground, it can be difficult to push the planter in deep enough and it can easily bend or break with repeated use.

1

2

3

4

5

Growing bulbs in pots

You don't have to plant bulbs in the ground to enjoy them in your garden. Containers planted with bulbs make a wonderful display and you can have different containers planted up for flowers at different times of year. One container can have a mix of bulbs to create a succession of flowers. If your garden soil isn't suitable for bulbs, you can grow them in containers filled with appropriate potting compost. This versatility has made growing bulbs in containers very popular and there is no reason not to have some bulbs growing in your garden, even if only in a window box or hanging basket.

◀ *Tulipa* 'Synaeda King' growing in a pot on a garden terrace

▲ Pots of autumn bulbs on display in the Davies Alpine House at Kew

Bulbs grown in pots can be displayed on a garden terrace when in flower, or placed by the front or back door of the house. When they have finished flowering, the pots can be moved out of sight, put under cover and allowed to dry off, giving the bulbs their dry dormant period. Alternatively, you can tip the bulbs out once they have died down and store them in a cool, dry, dark place until you are ready to plant them again.

A deep, wide container is best for growing bulbs, as this provides plenty of soil for the roots to grow down into and provides the nutrients that the bulbs need to build up food reserves for the following year. If you are not going to keep the bulbs after they have flowered, you can grow them in almost anything.

A loam-based soil like John Innes is ideal or you can buy specially mixed bulb compost. The container should have drainage holes to allow excess water to drain out of the soil. Cover the hole with pieces of broken pot or plastic netting to prevent soil falling through and fill the container to about half its depth with the soil. Arrange the bulbs on the soil and then cover them to just below the rim of the container. Tap the container firmly to settle the soil.

In a mixed pot, the larger bulbs, like tulips and daffodils, should be planted deeper, with smaller bulbs above them. Don't worry too much about planting at a depth 3 times the height of the bulb, as you would in the garden. It is more important to make sure there is enough soil below the bulbs for the roots to grow into. You can plant the bulbs close together, as long as they don't touch, but when planting in layers don't plant one bulb directly above another.

Once planted, give the bulbs plenty of water so all the soil is wet and you see water draining out of the hole in the base of the pot. Let the soil dry out a little before watering again but once you can see growth above ground, keep the soil moist until the bulbs begin to die down. Once dormant, plant the bulbs in the garden or reuse them in a new container display, using fresh soil.

◀ **Planting up a pot of bulbs**

Cross-section of a pot of mixed bulbs showing planting depths
▼

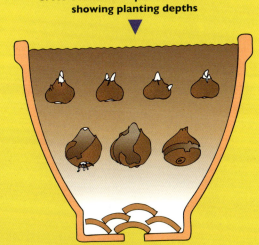

Long-term care

The majority of common garden bulbs can be planted and then left alone to flower year after year. The most important aspect of their long-term care is to make sure that the leaves are allowed to die down naturally so that all the nutrients can be withdrawn into the bulb. Avoid tying the leaves in knots to keep them tidy as this will reduce their ability to photosynthesise and build up nutrients for the following year. Once the leaves are completely brown, they can be cut off. Don't pull them unless they come away freely because you might end up pulling out the centre of the bulb, where next year's bud is formed. If the bulbs are planted in a lawn, only cut the grass once the bulbs' leaves have died down.

One problem that can occur in established clumps is a reduction in the number of flowers, caused by the bulbs becoming too congested and competing for nutrients in the soil. This is most often seen in old clumps of daffodils and snowdrops, and the solution is to lift them and spread them out. Wait until the leaves are starting to brown and dig up the whole clump. Separate the bulbs and replant straight away over a wider area, or use some to create a new patch elsewhere. Water the newly re-planted bulbs to settle the soil and give moisture to the still-active roots.

Another option for starved bulbs is to feed them. Use a low-nitrogen feed like bone meal or blood, fish and bone, sprinkled lightly over the ground around the bulbs and raked in. When it rains, the nutrients will be washed down through the soil to where the bulbs' roots can reach them. It is more likely that you will need to feed bulbs that are planted in pots, where the volume of soil is limited. You can use low-nitrogen plant food, like tomato feed, mixed with water and applied when the bulbs are in growth. Regular plant food should be avoided as it is high in nitrogen, which can encourage leafy growth at the expense of flowers. Feed once a month in the growing season to build up strong healthy bulbs. If you re-plant the bulbs every year in fresh pots of soil, feeding is less important but it is still worthwhile and will give you stronger plants.

◀ **Alliums often flower at the very end of their growing season, so by the time the flowers have finished, the leaves are already going brown or might have died down completely**

Pests and diseases

One reason bulbs are popular as garden plants is their reliability. Most commonly grown varieties come up year after year with few problems, but there are a few pests and diseases to look out for. In the garden, slugs and snails can eat newly emerging shoots and you may find rabbits or deer munching away at the top growth, just as you were anticipating a fine display of flowers. Garden bulbs are, however, largely free of serious disease if you grow them in a suitable position.

Heavy soil that is wet all year and a damp, humid atmosphere will encourage fungal diseases, and bulbs can rot away or their leaves become marked with spots or lesions, leading to distorted growth and eventual death. If your bulbs are wiped out by a fungal disease, it is advisable not to plant the same type of bulb in the same location for at least 3 years.

Soil with good drainage and an open position, with free air movement, is often enough to keep bulbs healthy but there are other pests that can afflict bulbs and need to be dealt with.

◄ A tulip with the fungal disease tulip fire, which distorts and discolours the leaves and flowers, and will kill the plant in a year or two

Aphids

Sap-sucking insects, also called greenfly or blackfly. They feed on young growth, distorting leaves and buds. More of a problem on bulbs that grow in late spring and summer, when aphids reproduce rapidly and can smother a plant. Squash between your fingers as soon as they appear or buy a spray if they get out of control. Aphids can spread virus between bulbs.

Mealy bugs

Usually found hidden away in the dry outer layers of the bulb or at the base of the leaves. They look like miniature woodlice or pill bugs but covered in white powdery wax. Often not a problem outdoors but can appear in pots of bulbs that are stored over the summer. Methylated spirit painted onto the bugs will break down their waxy coating and kill them.

Lily beetle

Attractive, bright red adults but the larvae are disgusting, covered in their own excrement as they eat the lily's leaves. Squash the adults if you catch them quickly; they tend to fall and land on their backs, exposing their black underside as camouflage against the soil. Not a problem everywhere, but they are spreading.

Adult lily beetle ▼

Propagation

Bulbs will naturally increase themselves by dividing underground. A single bulb may split in two, or small bulbs, called offsets or bulbils, may form around the base of the main bulb and eventually grow to flowering size. This can take several years but there are various ways to speed up the process. Alternatively, you can collect and sow seed to generate large numbers of seedlings that can be planted in the garden.

As bulbs increase naturally, they can become congested. These clumps can be lifted as they die down and the bulbs spaced out to give them more room and access to more nutrients. This will encourage them to divide further and you will gradually have more and more bulbs in your garden. This is especially effective with snowdrops, which can become quite congested within just a few years.

If you dig bulbs up or tip them out of a pot, you may find small bulbils attached to the main bulbs. These can be separated and potted up or re-planted to grow on. To promote the formation of more of these bulbils, the base of the bulb can be cut. The base of a bulb is called the basal plate and it is where the roots grow from. By cutting a shallow notch in this basal plate, new bulbils can be encouraged to form along the cut in a few weeks. After cutting, let the base dry and then plant the bulb in a small pot so that it is poking out of the top or keep it in a bag of damp soil. Check it every week or two to see if bulbils have formed. Separate these tiny bulbs and plant in their own pot to grow them on.

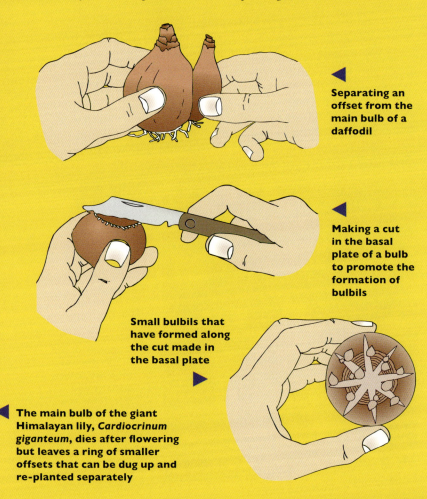

◄ **Separating an offset from the main bulb of a daffodil**

◄ **Making a cut in the basal plate of a bulb to promote the formation of bulbils**

Small bulbils that have formed along the cut made in the basal plate ▶

◄ **The main bulb of the giant Himalayan lily, *Cardiocrinum giganteum*, dies after flowering but leaves a ring of smaller offsets that can be dug up and re-planted separately**

Lily bulbs are different in that they are made up of many narrow, fleshy scales. Healthy, plump scales can be carefully pulled away from the bulb. Let the broken surface dry for a day and then put the scales in a bag of damp, but not wet, soil or vermiculite and keep them somewhere dark and warm. Roots can grow on these scales in a couple of weeks and then each scale can be potted up. They will still take a two or three years to reach flowering size.

◀ **Separating scales to propagate a lily bulb**

A tulip seed pod splitting open as it dries

The flat, wing-like seeds of *Cardiocrinum giganteum*

It can take four years or more to grow a flowering bulb from seed but it is the simplest way to produce large numbers of plants. After flowering, look out for the seed pods, and as they go brown they will start to split open. This is the time to harvest the seed by cutting off the seed pod and opening it up, or by placing them in a paper bag to catch the seed as the pod naturally splits open as it dries. Not all bulbs will produce viable seed because the breeding process that creates different garden forms means that they can be sterile. This is often the case with tulip and daffodil cultivars, but there are plenty of other bulbs that will produce good seed.

Some bulbs, like alliums, make attractive seed heads held well above the ground, whereas others, like crocus, will keep their seed pods at ground level and you will have to search around for them among the dying leaves. The seeds might be small, round and black, like tiny peppercorns, or large and flat, stacked like the leaves of a book in the plump seed pod. Collect them and dry them off before sowing in autumn or winter.

Sow the seed on the top of a pot of soil mix and cover with a thin layer of sieved soil. Water carefully and keep the soil moist. The pot can be left in a shaded, sheltered position outside, on the windowsill of a cool room or in cool glasshouse. When the seed germinates, most bulbs grow thin, grass-like leaves. Don't prick out the seedlings as you would seedlings of other plants but leave them in their pot to allow them to grow a small bulb before disturbing them. This can take a year or two. Then when the seedlings are dormant, tip them out and pot the little bulbs up into a larger pot. A couple of years later, they should be big enough to plant in the garden.

Some seed can be sown direct in the garden, in the position in which you want them to grow. *Tulipa sprengeri* and *Cyclamen coum* are two good examples of plants that are easily established this way and there are plenty of others. You may find that some bulbs do this anyway, naturally spreading themselves through a border.

Bulbs by Season

- Main Flowering Season
- Main Planting Season for dormant bulbs

	January	February	March	April	May	June	July	August	September	October	November	December
Snowdrops												
Crocus (spring)												
Eranthis												
Cyclamen coum												
Iris reticulata												
Daffodils												
Tulips												
Hyacinths												
Fritillaries												
Muscari												
Scilla												
Chionodoxa												
Erythronium												
Anemone												
Allium												
Lilium												
Camassia												
Gladiolus spp.												
Gladiolus cultivars												
Begonia												
Colchicum												
Crocus (autumn)												
Cyclamen (autumn)												
Sternbergia												
Nerine												

Introduction

The rest of this book is arranged by flowering season. From snowdrops in winter to colourful nerines in autumn, an array of flowering bulbs can be enjoyed in the garden all year round. When you plant bulbs is determined by when they have their natural growing season. They are usually best planted towards the end of their dormant season but there are slight variations, which are shown in the chart here. For example, bulbs that like a long, dry dormant season, like tulips, can be planted late in the autumn but those that do better if not allowed to dry out too long, like snowdrops, should be planted earlier. The chart shows timings based on planting dry dormant bulbs; if you buy bulbs that are growing in pots, you can plant them in the middle of their growing season.

▲ Autumn: hardy cyclamen, *Cyclamen hederifolium*

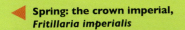

◀ Spring: the crown imperial, *Fritillaria imperialis*

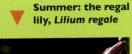

▼ Summer: the regal lily, *Lilium regale*

▲ Winter: the common snowdrop, *Galanthus nivalis*

Winter

Snowdrops

A cluster of delicate snowdrops glistening in the sunshine can lift the spirits in the middle of a long cold winter. They push through the ground, braving frost and snow, to produce their white blooms, subtly marked with dashes of green. Once established in a garden, snowdrops can spread to create flourishing colonies under trees, along hedgerows or scattered through a lawn or border. They appear when little else is growing and then, not wanting to outstay their welcome, they disappear again, hiding underground to leave the garden to its spring and summer display.

◀ *Galanthus nivalis*

▼ **A clump of the common snowdrop, *Galanthus nivalis*, growing through the fallen leaves of deciduous trees**

Snowdrops are members of the genus *Galanthus* and it may surprise you to know there are around 20 different species found in the hills and mountains of Europe and western Asia. Superficially similar, the different species show variation in their leaves, which can be broad and shiny or narrow and matt, bright green or blue-grey. The flowers differ in size and the green markings on the inner cup of petals also vary in size and shape. The different snowdrop species also vary in flowering time, with some appearing in the middle of winter and others waiting for early spring. There are even a couple of species that flower in autumn. In gardens, any slight difference leads to a new name being given to the selected form and there are many hundreds of cultivar names for the multitude of selections and garden hybrids. Some have no green markings at all, others have green on the outer as well as the inner petals and some can have yellow markings instead of green. These seemingly endless variations can be fascinating to some, and snowdrop collectors, known as galanthophiles, will fill their garden with every different form they can find.

Galanthus elwesii, the two green marks on the inner petals have joined to form a fish-like shape

Species to plant

If all you want is a glorious winter show of snowdrops, then there is no better plant than the common snowdrop, *Galanthus nivalis*. Individual plants will only grow to around 10 cm tall, but planted in a group, they can make a wonderful display that gradually spreads through a border or lawn. There is a double form, called 'Flore Pleno', and although this is not as pretty as the common form when viewed close up, its wider flowers can make more of an impact from a distance. If you want something a bit taller and more robust-looking, then plant G. elwesii, a Turkish species with blue-grey, channelled leaves and larger flowers. It grows to 20 cm tall and can have two green marks on the inner petals, one at the tip and one at the base, or marks that join together in the middle. Midway in size between these two species is G. woronowii, which has bright green, shiny leaves and dainty little flowers.

Galanthus woronowii, recognised by it shiny green leaves, on sale at an early-spring flower show

19

Garden cultivars

When different species of snowdrop are planted in a garden, it is highly likely that they will cross pollinate and create the plethora of hybrids beloved by galanthophiles. Even minor variants found within a single species are selected out and given a name. If you want to see a range of different types, then find an early-spring flower show where there might be stands devoted just to snowdrops. It is captivating to see all these different snowdrops together, showing such variation on a simple theme.

Some snowdrop cultivars, such as 'Atkinsii' and 'S. Arnott', make excellent, strong garden plants, whereas others are still uncommon and you can pay a hefty price for a single flowering bulb.

The large flowered *Galanthus* 'John Gray'

Galanthus 'Atkinsii'

A healthy colony of snowdrops from bulbs planted 'in the green'

Planting snowdrops

Snowdrops die down in spring and do not reappear above ground until the following winter, but they are not bulbs that need very dry soil during their dormant season. Bulbs bought in late summer and planted in the garden may not grow at all. This is because they have been out of the ground for too long and have dried out so much that they cannot recover. Snowdrops do best in soil that retains some moisture in the ground all year, which is why they do well in a lawn or in normal border conditions, as long as the soil isn't waterlogged. If you do buy dormant bulbs, try to get them as soon as they appear in the shops, so that they have not been allowed to dry out too much.

Another way to buy snowdrops is 'in the green'. This means when they are still growing. The plants are dug up as clumps when still in leaf, after flowering, and delivered for immediate planting. This ensures that they are as healthy as possible. The practice of planting in the green has been questioned, however, as damaging the delicate roots by digging them up when in growth can set the bulbs back for a year – they might be weakened and not flower the following year, but at least they are still alive. One of the best colonies of *G. nivalis* I know was planted in the green, by cutting slits in a lawn with a spade, and planting the still-growing bulbs into the soil. Over the years, they have gradually built up in numbers and now make a fine display every year. The ideal method is to dig up the bulbs when they are dormant and re-plant them straight away. This is possible in your own garden but when buying bulbs it may not be a realistic option, unless you can find a supplier who will damp-pack the bulbs and ship soon after lifting. The only other way is to buy them in pots and plant them out once they have died down, but this is an expensive way to acquire large numbers of plants.

The snowflakes

The snowflakes, members of the genus *Leucojum*, are a group of bulbs that are related to snowdrops and with similarly white flowers with green or yellow markings. They tend to flower later in the season but early forms might coincide with the last snowdrops. Their white petals, with a green tip, are all the same length and form downward-facing bells. The spring snowflake, *L. vernum*, can have yellow instead of green tips to the petals and flowers from early to mid spring. It grows around 20–30 cm tall. *Leucojum aestivum* is taller, to 60 cm, and known as the summer snowflake, but it too can flower in early spring. Snowflakes and snowdrops require similar conditions in the garden.

Collecting snowdrops in the wild

Owing to their popularity as garden plants, snowdrops have been extensively harvested from the wild for the horticultural trade in Europe and America. The international trade in snowdrops is now closely monitored under the rules of CITES (the Convention on International Trade in Endangered Species of Wild Fauna and Flora) to protect natural populations. Snowdrops can still be dug up from the wild and sold, but strict quotas are applied and permits are needed. Artificial propagation is encouraged to lessen the pressure on wild populations. Other bulbs covered by CITES include cyclamen and sternbergias.

Problems

Snowdrops are usually trouble-free once established in a garden. If they do disappear, this is more than likely because the ground is too wet, maybe after a particularly wet year, or because the soil has been compacted by repeated walking over the ground where the bulbs are planted.

If your bulbs seem healthy but do not flower well, it is a sign that they have become too congested. At the end of their growing season, lift the clump of bulbs and split them up, replanting them over a wider area. This gives the bulbs more soil to grow into, providing more nutrients and moisture and allowing the bulbs to build up the strength to flower again.

 Despite its name, the summer snowflake, *Leucojum aestivum*, can flower in early spring

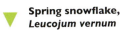 **Spring snowflake, *Leucojum vernum***

 **Bulbs of *Galanthus woronowii* cultivated in Georgia for export to Europe**

Crocus

Quickly following on from snowdrops, with some overlap in flowering time, are the spring crocus. In contrast to the snowdrop's subtle whites and greens, crocus provide a more colourful sign that spring is just around the corner. With flowers in shades of purple, violet, creamy white and yellow, they spring from the ground, making the most of any traces of warmth by opening their blooms wide in the sunshine. There are several species that are commonly available and many cultivars, some bred to form larger, more robust flowers. They are small plants, reaching only a few centimetres tall, but planted in broad swathes or left to naturalise, they create a stunning display of vibrant colour in a lawn or border.

Crocus grow from a corm and these are best planted in a sunny position in soil that isn't too wet in summer. They are often seen growing in a lawn, which suits them perfectly, or under deciduous trees, not in deep shade but along the edge of a woodland or shrub border, where they will still get some sun. Snowdrops make good companions to the early species like *C. tommasinianus*, but crocus corms are more drought tolerant than snowdrop bulbs and can be planted in drier situations. They are also better at surviving long periods in their packets on a garden centre shelf. The corms can be planted fairly deep, up to 10 cm down, but if planted too shallow they will pull themselves down with contractile roots so there should be no problem planting them under turf and leaving them to sort themselves out. Crocus corms do seem to attract mice and squirrels, which dig them up, so deeper planting might help with this problem.

The flowers are made up of six petals of which the outer three are frequently a different shade to the inner three and can have attractive patterning on the outer surface. Inside the flower is the style, which is sometimes intricately branched and often bright orange or yellow.

Crocus tommasinianus

One of the earliest crocus species to appear is *Crocus tommasinianus*. The flowers are bright lilac purple, and left to naturalise these plants will seed around and spread through a border. They can even be invasive in the right situation, but who can complain about the invasion of their garden by such a pretty flower? Plant clusters of corms and let them do their thing. The leaves follow the flowers and could be regarded as a little messy, but plant these bulbs among herbaceous perennials that grow to fill the space or under trees and there is little to worry about. *Crocus tommasinianus* are, however, at their best in a lawn, where they will cover the grass with their colourful blooms in late winter. Let them die down before cutting the grass. Cultivars like 'Whitewell Purple' and 'Barr's Purple' are selections of this species.

 Crocus tommasinianus

Crocus chrysanthus

This is a yellow-flowered species that appears in late winter and has been crossed with another species, *C. biflorus*, to create a range of cultivars. Some of these are pale violet blue, such as 'Blue Pearl', or creamy yellow as in 'Cream Beauty', but it is the rich yellow forms that make the best contrast with other species. 'Zwanenburg Bronze' and 'Gipsy Girl' are just two examples that have striking bronze or golden-yellow flowers.

▲ **Crocus chrysanthus 'Zwanenburg Bronze'**

Crocus vernus

Crocus vernus is an early-spring-flowering species that has been used to breed a range of large Dutch hybrids. These have rounded goblet-shaped flowers in white or shades of purple and violet, often with feathers of a darker colour on the outside of the petals. They are robust plants that can reach 12 cm tall and are suited to a range of garden situations or for planting in containers.

Large-flowered *Crocus* hybrids planted in grass ▶

The Chilean blue crocus, *Tecophilaea cyanocrocus*

These striking, intense blue flowers have a colour like nothing else in the bulb world. They appear in late winter and are usually seen growing in an alpine glasshouse, but they can survive outside in a sheltered spot. Well-drained soil and a sunny position are important, as well as a location that doesn't suffer from hard frosts. The flowers are similar in shape to those of a *Crocus* but despite its common name the Chilean blue crocus is not a true crocus; its Latin name is a bit of a mouthful, *Tecophilaea cyanocrocus*. For many years, this corm was thought to be extinct in the wild but it has been re-discovered in the Andes above the Chilean capital, Santiago.

◀ ***Tecophilaea cyanocrocus***

Other species to try

There are around 90 species of crocus but not all are suited to growing in the open garden. Those that can be tried include *C. sieberi*, from Greece, which has soft pale violet flowers, the inner petals paler than the outer, and a white or yellow throat. *Crocus sieberi* 'Tricolor' has violet flowers with a yellow throat edged with white. This species does best in free-draining soil and is well suited to a small rock garden. *Crocus corsicus*, from the Mediterranean island of Corsica, has violet inner petals and paler outer petals that are intricately patterned with purple on their outer surface.

▶ ***Crocus sieberi* subsp. *atticus* in a rock garden**

Winter aconite

Covering the ground with bright yellow flowers, the winter aconite, *Eranthis hyemalis*, looks best growing under shrubs or clustered around the base of deciduous trees. It seems well suited to normal garden conditions in northern Europe, despite coming from the warmer and drier climate further south. In fact, this plant is similar to the snowdrop in its dislike of a long drought in summer and does not cope well with conditions that are too hot and dry. Given a perfect environment of lightly dappled shade with some moisture in the soil all year round, the little winter aconite will soon start to spread.

Growing from a small, dark brown, knobbly tuber, each flower of the winter aconite is a lemon yellow chalice resting on a collar of bright green leaves that grows only a few centimetres above the ground. The flowers look like buttercups and it is no surprise to find that the genus *Eranthis* is in the same family as the buttercup. The most commonly grown species is *E. hyemalis*, which bursts through the soil in the middle of winter and makes a great companion for snowdrops or the winter-flowering *Cyclamen coum*.

Eranthis hyemalis can be grown in a lawn but it usually does best in a sunny to partially shaded border. The short stem holds the ruff of deeply-divided leaves, above which the single yellow flower opens. The flowers are followed by the green seed pods; a cluster of six follicles that split open to scatter the seeds being held within. Plant *Eranthis* tubers a few centimetres deep in the soil in early autumn and once established in a border the plants will begin to spread themselves by sowing their own seed.

Several cultivars are available and those in the Cilicica Group tend to have slightly larger flowers that open a little later than the species. *Eranthis* 'Guinea Gold' is a particularly fine cultivar in the Tubergenii Group, with large, golden yellow flowers. It is sterile so will spread more slowly as it doesn't produce seed. Double forms of *Eranthis* can be found but they lack the finesse of the single-flowered forms.

A cluster of the yellow winter aconite, *Eranthis hyemalis*

Cyclamen coum

Most species of cyclamen flower in spring or autumn, but there is one that is truly a winter star, the diminutive *Cyclamen coum*. Of all the winter bulbs that you can naturalise in your garden, it is a thriving carpet of *C. coum* that is most likely to take your breath away. Seen from a distance, the flowers merge to form a shimmering blanket of bright pink, but close up you can see the individual blooms, held on a short flower stem above the emerging circular leaves. Flower colour varies from palest pink to deepest magenta and they are very hardy, standing up to the frostiest conditions.

Cyclamen coum comes from the hills of Turkey, the Caucasus and Iran. In some of these places rainfall is extremely high and the tubers sit on rocky cliffs or in the walls of ancient ruins. In other locations this cyclamen will colonise a woodland floor, invade the edge of a field or nestle amongst the rocks on a river bank. In the garden it needs free-draining soil and a position that is not too hot or dry in summer. Under trees, in a sunny mixed border, among shrubs or on a rock garden are all places where you can easily grow *C. coum*.

Buy potted plants in bloom, so that you can see the colour of the flowers. Dormant tubers can be left out of the ground for too long and can suffer in the dry air of a shop or garden centre, so if you do buy dormant tubers, get them early and plant them as soon as possible. Don't plant the rounded tubers too deep in the soil. The leaves and flowers emerge from lumpy growing points at the top of the tuber and these should be at or very near the soil surface. The flowers open in the middle of winter, often before the leaves have fully expanded. Many cultivars are available with different combinations of flower colour and leaf patterning. The leaves are round to kidney-shaped and can be plain green or attractively marked with silvery patterns. Some forms, such as those in the Pewter Group, have entirely silver leaves. *Cyclamen coum* lasts through to late spring before dying down for the summer.

A carpet of *Cyclamen coum* at Wakehurst Place in Sussex, England

After flowering, the spherical seed pod develops as the stem begins to curl, bringing the seed down to ground level. The seeds are quite fleshy and attract ants, which pick up the seeds and move them around, helping to spread the plant through a border. One of the easiest ways to establish a good patch of this cyclamen is to sow seed direct onto the ground. Rake it in lightly and the first plants may flower after only a couple of years.

A magenta form of *Cyclamen coum* growing in a wall

The flowers may look delicate but they can withstand a hard frost

Reticulata irises

With flowers in shades of purple, violet, blue and yellow, the Reticulata irises bring a dash of unexpected colour to the winter garden. There are many different named forms and all you need to do is choose the colour you want and plant them in a border or a container. They grow from a bulb and are sold when dormant in the summer or as growing plants in winter. They are perfect for a pot, displayed on a terrace, in a porch or in a cool conservatory. You can squeeze quite a few into one container, 10 or 12 bulbs in a 15 cm diameter pot, and they will reward you with a dense cluster of flowers that all open together, brightening up the shortest, dullest days of the year.

Iris winogradowii

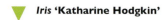

Iris **'Katharine Hodgkin'**

The flower of an iris is made up of three upright petals, called standards, and three lower, arching petals, called falls. *Iris reticulata*, which gives the group its name, has flowers in shades of violet, purple and blue. The standards are quite narrow and the falls are a little wider, with a tip often darker than the rest of the flower. In the centre of each fall is a pale zone, with a patterning of darker spots and blotches and a yellow to orange ridge down the centre. The leaves are narrow and triangular or quadrangular in section. Reticulata irises can be very short at flowering time, emerging just as the bud unfurls, but some forms are already quite tall when the flower opens and can reach 30 cm or more.

Species and cultivars

Although there are many cultivars, there are only a few species in the Reticulata group. They come from the hills and mountains of Turkey and the Middle East. The named forms you can buy are selections of individual species or hybrids from crosses made in cultivation, resulting in a range of flower colours. *Iris reticulata* is the best known species but *I. histrioides* has slightly larger flowers and they are normally a blue-violet colour with prominent blotches on the falls. *Iris winogradowii* is a beautiful yellow species whose flowers are pale primrose yellow and have relatively wide falls, intricately marked with faint veins and grey-green spots. It has been crossed with *I. histrioides* to create the hybrid *I.* 'Katharine Hodgkin'. The pale blue flowers of this iris are washed with yellow and each petal is delicately veined, with darker violet blotches on the falls.

Other cultivars to look out for include the pale blue 'Cantab', the deep purple 'George' and the royal blue 'Harmony'. The pale violet-blue flowers of 'Gordon' have a distinctive dark purple-blue tip to each fall and 'Alida' is a newer cultivar, with large, mid-blue flowers. For deep yellow flowers, you could try *I. danfordiae* but it doesn't tend to live long in the garden. Blue-flowered *I. histrio* is another species in this group that is better grown in a glasshouse, where it has a little more protection from the cold.

Iris **'George'**

Iris **'Harmony'**

Iris histrio, growing in an alpine house

Iris **'Alida'**

Planting Reticulata irises

The flowers of Reticulata irises are held 10–15 cm above the ground, which means they can be planted to emerge through the leaves of ground cover plants like ivy-leaved cyclamen or the black foliage of *Ophiopogon* 'Nigrescens'. They do not need a hot, dry summer, so partial shade and well-drained but moisture-retaining soil will suit them well. If they do get too dry, the bulbs can split into smaller bulbils that do not flower until they have grown for at least a couple of years. This is often a problem with these irises and deep planting is said to help prevent the bulbs dividing too much. Dig a hole 10 cm deep or more for planting and as long as the bulbs have enough moisture when they are in growth, then most should flower in subsequent years. If they are grown in pots, make sure that the bulbs do not dry out until completely dormant and give them some low-nitrogen feed while they are growing.

Spring

Daffodils

If you had to choose just one bulb to represent spring, then it would have to be a daffodil. When the daffodils are out, you know spring has well and truly arrived. These bright, sunny blooms appear in vast swathes in towns and villages up and down the country. They line the roads, march across lawns and cluster beneath trees, nodding in the breeze and basking in the sun, but they are able to stand up to all types of weather, seemingly determined to lighten our mood even if it is still pouring with rain and freezing cold.

Daffodils are members of the genus *Narcissus* and their natural habitat is southern Europe, especially Spain and Portugal, but they seem just as at home in gardens further north. It is their adaptability and reliability that have made them so popular and there are few gardens that can't accommodate some daffodils. The ideal time to plant the dormant bulbs is September or October, and they should be planted a good few centimetres deep, depending on the size of the bulb. Larger cultivars can be planted 15 cm down and the smallest forms 8–10 cm.

◀ ***Narcissus* 'February Gold' along the Broadwalk at Kew Gardens**

***Narcissus jonquilla* on a rock garden** ▶

Daffodils bulbs can be planted under deciduous shrubs and trees to give some early colour before they are shaded out. They are great in a lawn, where you can plants in clumps or broad sweeps, choosing one variety for impact or a mixture to lengthen the flowering season. A sunny position is best but dappled shade is also fine for most daffodils. They will naturally increase by producing offsets of their bulbs, slowly spreading or clumping up. Some daffodil species need better drainage and are more suited to a rock garden or a well-drained slope, but the majority of daffodils you can buy are suitable for general garden conditions; just avoid very wet or waterlogged ground.

The only downside to daffodils is the foliage. Their leaves can look tatty once the flowers are over but they should be left for around six weeks before being cut back, to allow the bulb to build up strength for the next year. If planted in a border, later flowering plants can hide the daffodils leaves but if they are in grass, you will have to let the grass grow tall before cutting. This is a small price to pay for those evocative spring flowers.

The daffodil flower

The typical daffodil flower is made up of six petals and a central cup or trumpet, called the corona. The corona varies in size and shape, from the long, majestic trumpets of large-flowered hybrids such as 'Dutch Master', to the short, delicate cup of the poet's narcissus, *N. poeticus*. These characteristics have been inherited from the wild species. The hoop petticoat daffodils, such as *N. bulbocodium* and *N. romieuxii*, have a wide, flaring corona and tiny, almost insignificant petals. In others, such as *N. cyclamineus*, the petals are swept back. Most of the larger daffodil hybrids have a single flower but there are many species that have multiple blooms. The popular winter-flowering paperwhite, *N. papyraceus*, is one example, as are *N. jonquilla* and *N. triandrus*.

The multi-flowered *Narcissus papyraceus* appears in winter

Narcissus bulbocodium, the hoop petticoat daffodil

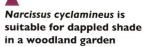

Narcissus cyclamineus is suitable for dappled shade in a woodland garden

Yellow is the colour usually associated with daffodils but whites are also popular. You can find bicoloured flowers, in which the corona is a lighter or darker shade than the petals, and more recent developments include shades of red, pink and orange appearing in the flower, particularly in the corona. These constant developments and improvements to the daffodil flower have resulted in over 27,000 cultivar names being registered. Although the range offered for sale is far smaller, there is still a huge number to choose from. To help you decide which ones to look out for, daffodil hybrids have been grouped into divisions, based on the flower type.

Daffodil divisions

There are thirteen divisions of daffodils, with the last being the wild species. The other twelve consist of hybrids and they are grouped according to flower shape or the species to which they are most similar.

Narcissus 'Thalia'

Narcissus 'Hawera'

The trumpet daffodil *Narcissus* 'Mount Hood'

Narcissus 'February Gold', a Cyclamineus cultivar that flowers early in the season

1 Trumpet daffodils
These have a trumpet as long or longer then the petals. 'Dutch Master' belongs here, as does the white-flowered 'Mount Hood'. These daffodils have a single flower per stem and can reach 50 cm tall

2 Large-cupped daffodils
Cultivars with a trumpet more than one third but less than equal the length of the petals. These also have a single flower.

3 Small-cupped daffodils
These have a single flower with a corona not more than one third of the length of the petals. They are often called 'narcissus' but strictly speaking all daffodils are in the genus *Narcissus*.

4 Double-flowered daffodils
In these daffodils, the corona is replaced with a bundle of overlapping petals, often of two colours. They may be single flowers or have up to five in a head.

5 Triandrus daffodils
Named after *N. triandrus*, a species with two or more small nodding flowers with reflexed petals. The cultivars have the same characteristic. They include 'Hawera', which can have up to eight pale yellow flowers and often more than one stem per bulb and the pretty 'Thalia', an old cultivar with nodding white flowers.

6 Cyclamineus daffodils
Also named after a species, *N. cyclamineus*, which has single flowers with petals that are strongly swept back. Cultivars in this group include the popular 'February Gold', an early flowering daffodil with golden yellow blooms on stems 30 cm tall. It is a great choice for growing in grass. Another good choice for grass is the shorter 'Jack Snipe', growing to 20 cm and with a yellow corona and swept back white petals.

7 Jonquilla daffodils
Named after *N. jonquilla*, which has several rounded, fragrant flowers per stem. The wonderful 'Sun Disc' grows to 20 cm and has perfectly round, miniature yellow flowers. It is best grown on a sunny bank or rock garden. The bicoloured 'Pipit' also belongs in this division, with lemon yellow petals and a corona that fades to white. It is a good choice for growing in grass or a border.

8 Tazetta daffodils
These can have up to 20 flowers per stem. They include the early flowering, scented paperwhite and cultivars such as 'Minnow' with a yellow corona and petals that fade to white. 'Golden Dawn' is deep yellow with an orange corona and does well in a border.

9 Poeticus daffodils
These have single, rounded flowers with white petals and a small cup in the centre, often with a red or orange rim. They flower late in the season and look good in grass under trees.

10 Bulbocodium daffodils
Also called the hoop petticoats, they have a characteristic wide flaring corona and tiny petals. They are small plants, growing 10–15 cm tall. There are a few cultivars but they make little improvement over species like *N. bulbocodium* itself, white *N. cantabricus* or the early *N. romieuxii*.

11 Split-corona daffodils
In the bizarre split-corona daffodils, the corona is cut to over half its length into segments that overlay the surrounding petals.

12 Other daffodils
This is a collection of cultivars that don't easily fit in the other divisions. The most notable daffodil here is 'Tête-à-tête', a very popular cultivar that is often sold flowering in pots in early spring but it does well in the garden too, in grass or border. More bulbs of 'Tête-à-tête' are grown than any other daffodil.

Narcissus 'Actaea', one of the Poeticus cultivars

Narcissus 'Minnow'

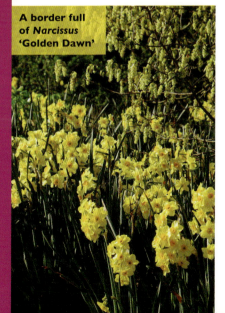

A border full of *Narcissus* 'Golden Dawn'

Narcissus romieuxii, an early-flowering Bulbocodium species

Tulips

And now it's show time! Forget the subtleties of winter snowdrops and the gentle yellows of spring daffodils, tulips are here to dazzle. Sturdy, upright stems holding goblets of shimmering red, candy pink, luscious purple, rich golden yellow and glistening white are the tulip's trademark. Plant them fresh and you will have bold blocks of uniform flowers rearing out of the ground at the height of spring. They are the choice of the formal gardener, filling bedding schemes with rigid patterns of colour, and of the adventurous gardener who dares to scatter them through a border. They are also great bulbs for containers. You can conjure up pleasing colour combinations, but tulips go with everything and nothing. They are one of the few plants in which clashing colours can work together. You can underplant them with other spring flowers, such as violas or forget-me-nots, but more often than not, the tulips will steal the show: you won't be looking at anything else.

The key with most tulips is to plant new bulbs every year. They have been bred to produce the uniformity of flower size, colour and height that makes them such good spring bedding plants. The following year, the flowers will be smaller and the stems uneven in length. Gradually, they will fade and disappear. There are some cultivars that will persist if left in the garden but if you want a natural-looking swathe of tulips, you will have to plant the species and they mostly need free-draining soil and plenty of sun.

Tulip species are plants of the Middle East and Central Asia, where the summer is long, hot and dry. In more northerly gardens, they will not do well in the damp, cool summers and this is one reason why many tulip cultivars don't hang around for more than a year or two. You can help by lifting the bulbs at the end of spring and storing them somewhere dry for the summer. Choose the biggest bulbs for replanting. Tulip bulbs don't mind being kept out of the ground for a long time, so they can be planted as late as November and even December without harm, around 10–15 cm deep.

There are a couple of diseases to look out for if you grow tulips. One is virus, which is spread by aphids, causing streaking on the leaves and flowers and weakening the plant. Kill the aphids to stop it spreading and destroy affected plants. The other is tulip fire, a fungal disease that can wipe out a tulip collection in a year. First appearing as spots on the bulb, leaves and flowers, it distorts growth and kills the plant. An open, airy position helps to prevent tulip fire. Again, destroy any infected plants and don't plant tulips in the same place for three years.

◀ Tulips in a spring bedding display

Tulipa kaufmanniana ▶

Tulip cultivar groups

Like daffodils, tulip cultivars are classified in groups. Three of the groups are named after species and the cultivars are those most closely resembling the wild plants from which they have been bred. Some of the earliest to flower are in the Kaufmanniana Group, which resemble the species *Tulipa kaufmanniana*, also called the water lily tulip. They have funnel-shaped flowers that open close to the ground above wide leaves. They can be red, orange, yellow or white and many have contrasting colour on the outside of the petals and markings inside the flower. The Greigii group are similar but flower later. They often have attractive maroon-purple stripes and dashes on the leaves. The Fosteriana group contains cultivars that are similar to *T. fosteriana*. This species has bright red, shiny flowers and wide grey-green leaves. The cultivars, such as 'Red Emperor' and the white 'Purissima', can live for several years in the garden.

The other cultivar groups are based on flowering time and flower shape. Double-flowered tulips are divided between the Double Early and Double Late groups. Single Early tulips, like 'Apricot Beauty', grow 20–40 cm tall and flower in late March and April. Single Late tulips, such as the popular, dark purple 'Queen of Night', can reach 60 cm tall and flower in late April and May. Triumph tulips are similar to Single Early tulips but flower in mid season and are a little taller. There are many fine tulips in this group, such as plum red 'Couleur Cardinal' and 'Prinses Irene', which has orange flowers flamed with reddish-purple on the outer petals. The Darwin Hybrid tulips have magnificent, wide bowl-shaped flowers in the whole range of tulip colours.

The Lily-Flowered Group contains some of the most elegant tulips, such as orange 'Ballerina', yellow 'West Point' and 'White Triumphator'. The flowers of these tulips are vase-shaped, with a narrow waist and pointed tips. The Parrot tulips, such as 'Rococo', have deformed, contorted petals that look better than they sound! Fringed tulips have frilly edges to their petals and the Viridiflora Group includes cultivars that have petals flushed with green on the outside, such as 'Spring Green'.

Tulipa **'Couleur Cardinal' from the Triumph Group**

The Lily-Flowered *Tulipa* **'Ballerina'**

Tulipa **'Love Song', a member of the Kaufmanniana group**

Tulip species

If you want tulips in your garden that will stay and flower every year, you need to plant the species. They need plenty of sun and soil that is well drained to do well. The exception is *Tulipa sprengeri*, which can be grown in dappled shade and will seed around to create a colony of bright scarlet blooms in a few years.

There are around 80 species of tulip and many will not survive in the garden, but those that do include the low-growing *T. urumiensis* (usually sold as *T. tarda*), which has bright starry flowers that are yellow or white with a yellow centre. Red-flowered species include the resilient, multi-flowered *T. praestans*. *Tulipa clusiana*, the lady tulip, has white flowers brushed with reddish-pink on the outer petals. It also comes in yellow and there are a few cultivars of this species that show slight variations in colour. Another species with several cultivars is *T. linifolia*, which can be creamy white, bronze, apricot or red. *Tulipa saxatilis* 'Lilac Wonder' has pink flowers with a yellow centre, and one of the best species tulips for the garden is the bright yellow *T. sylvestris*, which can spread by underground stolons to form a colony.

▲ A red form of *Tulipa linifolia*

▼ The lady tulip, *Tulipa clusiana*

▼ *Tulipa urumiensis* is usually sold under the name *T. tarda*

Tulip Breaking Virus and tulipomania

We now know that a virus was responsible for the gloriously striped and feathered tulips seen in seventeenth-century Dutch flower paintings, but at the time the cause of these characters was a mystery. The unpredictability of the patterning only added to their allure. This led to the famous Tulipomania period in 1630s Holland, when infected bulbs attained almost mythical status and exchanged hands for huge sums of money. The bubble burst and money was lost but the tulips lived on. In the nineteenth century, these 'English florist's tulips' were exhibited by florists' societies across England, but today, only the Wakefield and North of England Tulip Society survives to carry the flame for these bizarre blooms.

Hyacinths and bluebells

A bowl of hyacinths is a traditional Christmas gift, but these bulbs have been forced to flower early and if you plant them out in the garden they will flower the following spring. Like tulips, the various cultivars of hyacinth are great for bedding. They are uniform in shape and colour and make an eye-catching display alongside pansies and polyanthus. Planted in a less formal setting, they can be hard to place effectively. The dense, cylindrical flower heads look far removed from any wild relatives, even a little artificial. In a container, on the other hand, they can look fantastic, and they have an intoxicating fragrance.

Hyacinth cultivars have been bred from the species *Hyacinthus orientalis* and their flower colours are mostly shades of blue, pink and white. There are yellow hyacinths too, such as 'Yellow Queen' and 'City of Haarlem'. 'Hollyhock' is crimson red and 'John Bos' is rose red. The colour of many hyacinths is obvious from the name, such as 'Delft Blue', 'Blue Jacket', 'White Pearl' and 'Pink Angel'. They all require similar treatment, whether grown in the garden, container or window box. Plant the bulbs so that the top is about 5 cm below ground. In a shallow container, hyacinth bulbs can be planted just below the surface. They will even flower without soil with just a supply of water. Balance the bulb on a jar so that the roots grow down into the water. After flowering, these bulbs will be very weak and probably not worth keeping as they have had none of the nutrients required to build up strength for the next year, but this is a novel way of displaying the scented flowers indoors.

▲ **A woodland carpeted with bluebells in spring**

◀ **A display of hyacinth cultivars at the RHS Chelsea Flower Show**

 A pink hyacinth planted in an informal border

 The Spanish bluebell, *Hyacinthoides hispanica*, has pale blue flowers on straight stems

Bluebells

The English bluebell, *Hyacinthoides non-scripta*, is closely related to the hyacinth. One of the glories of the British native flora is a woodland carpeted with masses of shimmering bluebells in late April or early May. Their arching stems, 20–30 cm tall, hold deep violet-blue, dangling bells. They should not be confused with the Spanish bluebell, *Hyacinthoides hispanica*, which is more vigorous and often seen in suburban gardens. It will out-compete the English bluebell, so should not be introduced to natural habitats where native bluebells grow. The Spanish bluebell can be easily distinguished by its paler blue flowers that are held all around the flower stem, not hanging from one side.

Fritillaries

One of the most impressive spring bulb species is the magnificent *Fritillaria imperialis*, the crown imperial. Deep orange or yellow bells hang in a cluster at the top of a sturdy stem that can grow a metre tall and is topped off with a tuft of narrow leaves. In stark contrast, many other species in the genus *Fritillaria* are small plants, with their bell-shaped flowers in shades of dusky purple, yellow, brown and green, but with intricate markings on the inside that deserve a closer look. Then there is the beautiful snakes head fritillary, *F. meleagris*, a plant of seasonally flooded meadows across northern and eastern Europe, including Britain, where it famously grows in Magdalen College Meadows in Oxford. The flowers are a pale purple but delicately chequered with darker purple, and populations often have pure white forms mingled amongst them.

Fritillaria persica 'Ivory Bells'

The impressive crown imperial, Fritillaria imperialis

Most species of *Fritillaria* come from southern Europe, the Mediterranean region, Turkey, Iran and eastwards to Central Asia. The Central Asian fritillaries usually prefer a hot, dry summer but there are several species, particularly from Europe and Turkey, that can be grown successfully in the garden. A woodland border is ideal for some fritillaries, including *F. imperialis*, which will grow and flower while the trees are bare but will be kept fairly dry in summer as the trees draw excess moisture out of the soil. The bulbs of *F. imperialis* are large and have a distinctive 'foxy' smell. You'll notice it straight away. They should be planted around 15 cm deep or more. The smaller species can be planted only 6–10 cm deep, depending on size.

Fritillaria persica is another tall species, approaching a metre tall or more. Instead of a flower cluster at the top of the stem, it produces a tall spike of 20 or more dangling bells of greenish-brown to dusky purple. The cultivar 'Adiyaman' has dark purple flowers, whereas the flowers of 'Ivory Bells' are creamy green. *Fritillaria persica* does well in a sunny border.

The other species of *Fritillaria* that are suitable for the garden tend to be shorter, growing 20–40 cm tall and holding a single bloom or a loose cluster of flowers. Many of these smaller fritillaries are not brightly coloured, but their flowers are delicately patterned and have a special charm of their own. Good drainage and full sun are required for most, but there are a few that do well in a partially shaded border in soil that doesn't dry out completely.

 The snake's head fritillary, *Fritillaria meleagris*, growing in a meadow

Fritillaria pallidiflora has one of the largest flowers in the genus, which are broad, downward-facing cups of creamy greenish-yellow. Plant it in a cool spot under dappled shade. For a drier position in light shade, try *F. uva-vulpis* with its brownish-purple flowers that have a yellow tip to each petal, or *F. messanensis*, in which the reddish-purple flowers have a broad green stripe down the centre of each petal or in which the flowers can be almost entirely green. *Fritillaria acmopetala* has similar flowers and is an easy species for sun or dappled shade.

In a well-drained border or container, try the more colourful *Fritillaria michailovskyi*. This has rich purple flowers that look like they have had their tips dipped in yellow paint. It is quite short, growing to only 10–15 cm, so it is best planted in a small group at the front of a sunny border, where it can't be missed. If you have a raised bed, then even better, as you will be able to look at the flowers more easily and the improved drainage will allow you to grow a wider range of species.

For growing in a lawn, you can't beat the wonderful *Fritillaria meleagris*. Dappled shade or full sun are both fine for this plant, as long as the soil holds some moisture all year round. If conditions are suitable, it will begin to seed around so that when it blooms in April, you will have a glorious meadow of chequered purple and white flowers scattered through the grass.

***Fritillaria michailovskyi* needs good drainage and plenty of sun**

Small blue bulbs

Small and blue might at first seem an arbitrary way to group bulbs together, but there is a surprising number of spring bulbs that fit into this category. From 2001 to 2004 the Royal Horticultural Society ran a trial of 'small blue bulbs' to assess those most suitable for garden cultivation. Most species were in three genera, the grape hyacinths (*Muscari*), glory of the snow (*Chionodoxa*) and squills (*Scilla*). Small means under 30 cm tall and generally less than 20 cm tall. Blue can mean pale blue to deep blue but also shades of violet and lavender, as well as a few white forms of normally blue species. Most of these bulbs should be planted 7–10 cm deep, under turf or in a border.

Muscari

Probably the best known of these small blue bulbs are grape hyacinths, members of the genus *Muscari*. The flowers are tiny blue baubles clustered on the stem like an upward-pointing bunch of grapes. Each flower is made up of six petals fused together to leave just a small, outward-facing opening, sometimes with a white rim. The flower stem is leafless but long, narrow leaves grow from the base. In some forms, these can look messy once the flowers have faded so the trick is to plant them where the leaves will not be too obvious or swamp surrounding plants. They can be grown in grass, which hides the leaves or try them in dry soil under trees or shrubs, where little else will thrive.

Muscari armeniacum is a robust and variable species and several cultivars are available, such as the double-flowered 'Blue Spike' and the pale blue 'Jenny Robinson'. Cultivars of another species, *Muscari aucheri*, include 'White Snow', which has white flowers that open from greenish buds. Then there are the grape hyacinths with flowers in two shades of blue in each spike. 'Peppermint' and

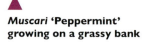

Muscari 'Peppermint' growing on a grassy bank

Muscari armeniacum

Muscari latifolium

'Mount Hood' are two examples in which the top flowers are pale blue and the lower flowers are much darker blue. There are many other variations to look out for, including pinks and sky blues, but one that doesn't have the problem of unruly foliage is *Muscari latifolium*. This has two wide leaves held up alongside the spike of blue flowers.

Scilla

On coastal cliffs along the west coast of Britain and south to the Iberian Peninsula grows the tiny spring squill, *Scilla verna*. Barely higher than the short turf it grows in, it displays a compact raceme of starry blue flowers in May. It is too small and insignificant for most garden situations but it has many relatives that make more of a show. One of the best is *S. sibirica*, including its cultivar 'Spring Beauty'. The nodding flowers are an intense blue and held on stems 10 cm tall in March. Later and much larger is *S. peruviana*, which holds a broad, stocky pyramidal head of similar starry blue flowers, above a rosette of pointed, lance-shaped leaves. Both species are well suited to a sunny border. *Scilla peruviana* flowers in May or early June and, growing to 30 cm tall, it can hold its own in a garden full of late spring perennials.

To create a carpet of blue in mid spring, plant *S. bithynica* in a partially-shaded border and watch it go. Once settled, it will gradually invade the space, producing flowers of bright blue in a mildly ramshackle way, making it more suited to wilder parts of the garden where it makes a great companion to the wood anemone. It can swamp a border with its leaves but they will disappear completely after a few weeks.

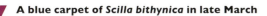

A blue carpet of *Scilla bithynica* in late March

▲ ***Chionodoxa siehei***

▲ ***Scilla sibirica* 'Spring Beauty'**

Chionodoxa

Like *Scilla bithynica*, the glory of the snow, *Chionodoxa*, can also make a spreading blue carpet but usually a little earlier in the spring. Although similar to the smaller squills, they can be distinguished by the flowers having a prominent white centre. They do best in a border but can also be naturalised in a lawn and because they flower early and die back fairly quickly, the grass doesn't have to be left to get too long before it can be cut.

There are just a few species and they all look quite similar, so the names are often mixed up. Those you are most likely to come across include *Chionodoxa siehei*, *C. forbesii*, *C. luciliae* and *C. sardensis*. There is not much to tell them apart; they all have bright blue flowers with a white centre. There are also pink and white forms, such as 'Pink Giant' and 'Alba'. *Chionodoxa luciliae* is said to have the largest flowers and they are a paler blue than most.

Dog's tooth violets

The erythroniums are the most elegant and refined spring bulbs you can grow. They deserve a more sophisticated common name than dog's tooth violet but it is descriptive, referring to the actual bulb, which is shaped like a canine tooth. They also deserve to be grown more frequently than they are, but their popularity is probably restricted by their need for a free-draining but humus-rich, woodland soil, under dappled shade: not every garden provides these conditions. If you can find a place for them, they are well worth trying. Plant 10–15 cm deep in random clusters through a border to give a touch of style to the spring display. Dormant bulbs don't like to dry out too much so plant them straight away or buy them damp-packed.

Erythronium revolutum

Erythronium 'Pagoda'

Erythronium dens-canis, the dog's tooth violet

The flowers are nodding but the petals are swept gracefully backwards, creating beautiful dancing flowers in shades of pink, violet, purple, yellow and creamy white, held above often mottled or marbled leaves. A few species of *Erythronium* grow in Europe and Asia but most species are North American. The European *E. dens-canis* was the plant originally called dog's tooth violet; *dens-canis* means tooth of a dog and the flowers are indeed violet. It is one of the shortest species of erythronium, growing to barely 10 cm tall.

The North American species are called trout lily or glacier lily and they show the greatest variation. They range from *E. grandiflorum* and *E. tuolumnense* (and the vigorous hybrid between them, 'Pagoda'), with their bright yellow flowers and plain green leaves, to *E. californicum* and its cultivar 'White Beauty', which have white blooms and marbled foliage. Pink and violet flowers are found in *E. revolutum* and *E. hendersonii*. All grow 20–40 cm tall. They are slow to increase but well worth the wait.

Anemones

There are many different types of *Anemone*, including rhizomatous species such as the wood anemone, *A. nemorosa*, and the tall autumnal Japanese anemones, which are classed as herbaceous perennials. A few species are from the Mediterranean region and die down for the summer. They grow from tubers or small rhizomes and appear from early spring. *Anemone blanda* and *A. apennina* have white or blue, daisy-like flowers and can be grown in sun or dappled shade, in humus-rich, leafy soil. *Anemone coronaria* and *A. pavonina* are taller, more brightly coloured and better for well-drained soil in full sun.

Anemone blanda grows from small knobbly tubers that should be planted just 3–5 cm deep. It likes a free-draining soil but can be grown in partial shade and does well under deciduous trees, where conditions can be fairly dry in summer but moist in winter and spring. The daisy flowers are usually blue or white but there are several cultivars including 'Pink Star' and 'Radar', which has bright magenta-pink flowers with a white centre. *Anemone apennina* is very similar but less widely grown. It grows from small, fat rhizomes and is a plant for the woodland garden that grows well under shrubs, in soil that doesn't dry out completely. It produces plenty of low, finely-divided leaves over which the flowers are held 10 cm or so above ground.

Anemone coronaria, sometimes called the poppy anemone or crown anemone, has flowers of bright scarlet to rich purple. Behind the flower on the stem is a ruff of small, finely-divided leaves. In the wild, *A. coronaria* grows on rocky slopes and in sunny meadows around the Mediterranean, so in the garden it will need good drainage and plenty of sun. The knobbly tubers are sold alongside other spring bulbs and should be planted around 5 cm deep. Among the cultivars available are those in the single-flowered De Caen Group and the double St Brigid Group. These are often sold as mixed colours, with flowers of red, purple, pink and white. *Anemone pavonina* has a few more petals in each flower and the leaves on the stem are less divided, but otherwise it is similar to *A. coronaria*. Both species grow to around 25 cm tall.

Anemone apennina growing with hellebores in a woodland border

Anemone coronaria growing in a Mediterranean meadow

Blue-flowered Anemone blanda

Summer

Alliums

The transition from spring to summer is marked by the flowering of the large ornamental alliums, with dramatic drumsticks that emerge from a border to sway above the sea of early summer perennials. Not all alliums flower at this time and not all are purely ornamental. Onions, leeks, garlic, shallots and chives are all in the genus *Allium*, but it is the 'ornamental onions' that are grown for their flowers. Among the hundreds of species from North America, Europe and Asia are plants that flower from spring through to autumn, but it is during late spring and early summer that the most impressive forms bloom, some reaching over a metre tall. These are flowering at the end of their growing season and the leaves have often begun to die back by the time the flowers open. Shortly after flowering, the plants go into their summer dormancy, but not before their flower heads dry out as the seeds mature, adding a final flourish before they disappear completely.

Allium subhirsutum has loose umbels of white flowers

Allium giganteum can reach over a metre tall

The allium flower

In most species of *Allium*, each individual flower is a small star, with six petals surrounding a central ovary. A few have more tubular flowers and they may be nodding, as in the American *A. cernuum* and the European *A. flavum*, but all are held on thin stalks that arise from a single point at the top of the main, leafless stem. The flowers form a loose cluster, a domed umbel or, more often, a completely round ball of flowers. Hundreds of flowers can be densely packed into a single flower head, which can reach over 20 cm across in the largest forms. The flower colour is more often than not a shade of purple, but among the many alliums to choose from are flowers of white, yellow, pink and blue. The main stem that holds the flower head ranges from a metre and a half tall, like that of *A. giganteum*, to only a few centimetres, like those of *A. akaka* and *A. karataviense*, which have a ball of flowers nestling between two wide, blue-green leaves, almost at ground level.

Selecting alliums for the garden

Your choice of *Allium* for the garden depends on the effect you want to create. For dramatic balls of flowers floating across a border, an increasing number of hybrids are available with large round flower heads, but you can't go wrong with 'Globemaster'. A dense head of purple flowers, of up to 20 cm across, is held on a thick sturdy stem that reaches 85 cm tall or more. The large bulbs can divide after the first year, so you will have more stems appearing but the flower heads will be a little smaller. Even taller is *A. giganteum*. In this species, the flower head is not as wide but this is a good thing, as it means that the plant doesn't become top heavy and fall over. There are fewer alliums that have white flowers to choose from, but 'Mount Everest' has a similarly large flower head on a tall stem.

Smaller species are usually easier to accommodate in a border, without it looking too much like some sort of fairground attraction. One of the most popular alliums is the reliable 'Purple Sensation' whose flower heads are 10 cm across and an intense, bright purple. This cultivar reaches 60–80 cm tall and combines well with early perennials such as geraniums, alchemillas and hostas. *Allium nigrum* is a similar size but with white flowers held in a domed umbel.

Even shorter is the wonderful *A. cristophii*. This plant has more open but stiff flower heads, up to 25 cm across. You can clearly see the structure of the umbel, with the wiry, red-tinged stalks holding each shimmering purple star, like miniature fireworks exploding in the garden. Growing just 45–60 cm tall, it needs to be planted near the front of a border and once flowering is over, the dried seeds heads linger. For smaller flower heads and shorter stems, there is a range of species and cultivars to choose from. *Allium caeruleum* is clear blue and *A. moly* 'Jeanine' is bright yellow. Then there is the garden designer's favourite, *A. sphaerocephalum*, with its small, dense flower heads of deep purple. It looks great with ornamental grasses.

▲ **Mighty *Allium* 'Globemaster' in a mixed border** ▲ **The more open flower heads of *Allium cristophii***

Planting alliums

The majority of alliums mentioned here are from hot dry places so they need well-drained soil and a sunny position. The giant hybrids are more tolerant, as long as the soil isn't too heavy or waterlogged. The smaller species and cultivars need light soil and care must be taken to avoid overcrowding them with big-leaved companion plants. Large bulbs, such as those of 'Globemaster', should be planted 15–20 cm deep and the smaller forms 7–10 cm. When spacing bulbs out, remember how wide the flower heads will be.

Lilies

Lilies are the classic summer bulb, flowering from early summer to the first days of autumn, but not all lilies look great in the garden. Many have been bred as cut flowers or to grow in pots, and their garish colours and oversized blooms look unnatural in a border. There are plenty of other lilies that do look good in a garden setting and their flowers range from small colourful 'Turk's caps', with reflexed petals, to gleaming trumpets with a heady fragrance. The conditions they require are as varied as the size and shape of the flowers, but generally they like sun with a cool root run. Plant them among summer perennials or shrubs to shade the ground they are growing in but allow the flowers to bask in sunlight. The bulbs are made up of a cluster of scales and should be planted 15–20 cm deep from autumn to early spring.

Lily species

Some of the best lilies for the garden are natural species. They belong to the genus *Lilium* and are plants of the temperate regions of the Northern Hemisphere, from North America through Europe and Asia to Japan. Many come from areas of high summer rainfall, such as the monsoon regions of the Himalaya and China, which is why they are summer growers. One of the most spectacular is the trumpet-flowered *Lilium regale*, from China. Glistening white trumpets, flushed with reddish-purple on the outside and with a yellow throat, are held aloft on tall leafy stems a metre or more in height. *Lilium regale* 'Album' lacks the reddish flush on the outside. *Lilium nepalense* is an unusual Himalayan species with downward-pointing trumpets of pale yellowish-green, darkly stained with rich maroon in the centre. It prefers acid soil and needs plenty of moisture when in growth, but if you have a sheltered, partially-shaded spot, it is worth a try.

▲ **Lily bulbs**

▲ *Lilium davidii*

Lilies with flowers that have recurved petals are often called Turk's caps and they include the Chinese species *Lilium henryi* and *L. davidii*. Both have nodding, orange flowers with darker spots towards the centre and anthers held out on long filaments. They are lime tolerant and ideal for a woodland garden or a partially-shaded border of humus-rich but well-drained soil. From Europe comes one of the easiest lilies for the garden, *L. martagon*. Its leaves are held in whorls on a stem that reaches over a metre tall and carries up to 50 small Turk's cap flowers. Colours range from deep plum purple to pale lilac and white.

▼ **The white, scented trumpets of the regal lily,** *Lilium regale*

Lilium pyrenaicum is a yellow-flowered Turk's cap species from the Pyrenees in France and Spain. Growing 50–75 cm tall, it can become naturalised in the garden in an open position and will grow in grass. The flowers open early in the summer. Even shorter is the eastern Asian *Lilium pumilum*, with bright scarlet Turk's cap flowers opening in midsummer on leafy stems of 40–50 cm tall. It needs some shade and a neutral to acid soil.

Flowering in late summer is the wonderful *Lilium speciosum*. Metre-tall stems carry an array of large white, scented flowers with recurved petals that are heavily spotted with dark pink. Often said to need acid soil, this species can grow in neutral soil and a sunny position as long as the roots are kept cool. Coming from eastern China and Japan, it is classed as one of the 'Oriental lilies', along with another stunning species, the golden-rayed lily, *L. auratum*.

The golden-rayed lily, *Lilium auratum*

Lilium pumilum

Lilium pyrenaicum

A dark-flowered form of *Lilium martagon*

Lilium speciosum

Hybrid lilies

By far the greatest number of lilies offered for sale in catalogues and garden centres are hybrids. The various species have been selected and crossed to bring out new colours and forms. These hybrids are grouped into eight divisions and the most common are the Asiatic Hybrids, the Trumpets and the Orientals.

▲ *Lilium* 'Minos', an Asiatic lily hybrid

Asiatic lilies are easy to grow and have large star-like flowers in many different colours. Some have been bred to produce outward- or upward-facing flowers. Short-stemmed forms are best for pots and others are specifically grown for cut flowers. Their bright colours need to be placed carefully to avoid any glaring clashes of colour.

Trumpet lilies are like the regal lily but come in many colours, from deep purple to yellow, orange and red. They can grow in acid or alkaline soil and make fine plants for a large container.

The Oriental hybrids are derived from species such as *Lilium speciosum* and *L. auratum* and, like those lilies, they flower towards the end of summer and have fragrant flowers. They will do best in acid soil. Their flowers can be trumpets, saucers or large Turk's caps, depending on which of the species they are closest to.

Lilies in pots

Lilies are excellent bulbs for containers, in which the soil can be adapted to meet the plant's needs. Plant them in an open, free-draining soil mix, adding ericaceous compost if growing the acid-loving Oriental lilies. Mix in a little fine grit or sand and, if using loam-based compost, add some well-rotted organic matter, such as garden compost. Plant the bulbs half-way down the pot, making sure they are not too crowded; three good-sized bulbs will need a pot of at least 30 cm in diameter. Don't let the soil dry out and keep watering after flowering until the leaves begin to die down.

The giant Himalayan lily

The biggest bulb you are likely to come across in a garden is the towering giant Himalayan lily, *Cardiocrinum giganteum*. It can reach over 2 metres tall, with its wide, glossy leaves forming a broad rosette on the ground and clothing the stem as it reaches for the sky. At the top of the stem, the long white trumpets open in a loose raceme in June or July. After flowering, the fat green seed pods develop and as they dry out, they split open to reveal the neat stacks of flat seeds.

The massive bulb takes seven years or more to reach flowering size from seed. Then, once it has flowered it dies. All is not lost because around the main bulb are offsets that take over and will flower themselves within a few years. Plant the bulb near the surface, so the tip is just covered, in humus-rich soil under cool, dappled shade.

▼ *Cardiocrinum giganteum* growing with blue *Meconopsis* in a woodland border

Camassia

You could argue that camassias are spring bulbs but they flower very late in that season, in May and June, which really makes them early summer bulbs. They are related to hyacinths and bluebells but are larger, displaying blue or white flowers on spikes from 40 cm to over a metre tall, depending on the species. They should be planted in a sunny position but they are tolerant of a range of soils and are good for heavy, damp ground where few other bulbs will thrive. They make a great display in grass, the wands of blue wafting in the breeze, but the grass will have to be left to get very tall before the camassias have died down and it is a safe to cut.

Like the alliums that flower around the same time, camassias bloom at the end of their growing season so their long, strap-like leaves can look tatty when the flowers are out. Growing in grass can hide the leaves, but in a border it is advisable to plant them behind something that will obscure the foliage. They look good in a border, clumped together and flowering through low-growing perennials and you don't have to worry about providing especially well-drained soil. Plant the bulbs 15–20 cm deep in autumn.

Camassias come from North America, where they grow wild in the Pacific Northwest and are often called camas lilies or quamash. Three species are commonly offered for sale. *Camassia cusickii* is the first to flower, so early that it can be used as a final blast in spring bedding. The flowers are pale blue on stems 60 cm tall and the cultivar 'Zwanenburg' has slightly darker flowers. This species is good for growing in grass too. *Camassia leichtlinii* is white or blue-flowered and is the tallest camassia, reaching 70 cm to a metre or more, with the blues ranging from violet to dark blue. *Camassia quamash* is the shortest species and is another good one for grass, reaching 30 or 40 cm and displaying intense blue flowers.

Camassia cusickii 'Zwanenburg'

Gladiolus

Summer gladioli belong to another group of plants that have been so manipulated and interbred in cultivation that the resulting plants are difficult to integrate into a garden, unless you are growing them in a designated corner of your plot, specifically for cutting. There are more refined forms, closer to the wild species, that make a valuable contribution to a sunny border or gravel garden and these are the ones to choose if you want to maintain some degree of good taste. On the other hand, if you are willing to abandon good taste altogether then the hybrid gladioli are just the plants for you.

Most species of *Gladiolus* are from South Africa but a few species grow in the Mediterranean region and these are the ones to try in the garden, mixed with alliums and aromatic shrubs of lavender, salvias and rosemary. They grow from corms that should be planted around 7–10 cm deep in free-draining soil and full sun. They flower in late May or early June. *Gladiolus communis* subsp. *byzantinus* and *G. italicus* are similar but the latter has paler pink flowers, whereas the former's flowers are striking magenta pink and held on thin stems 60–80 cm tall, enveloped at the base by the sword-like leaves. They can also be grown in a meadow, which is how you will find them in the wild.

The numerous South African species are showy but not reliably hardy and these have had a major influence in the breeding of *Gladiolus* hybrids, which are also not hardy enough to leave in the ground over winter. These hybrids flower in July and August

▼ **Gladiolus communis subsp. byzantinus in a gravel garden**

▼ **Gladiolus 'May Bride'**

and have large, blousy flowers. Some are quite tasteful, such as the pure white 'May Bride' but plenty are harsher in colour and some are bicoloured, like 'Princess Margaret Rose'. The heavy blooms mean that the stems need staking to prevent them falling over but they do make amazing cut flowers. Lift the corms in autumn and store in a frost-free environment until the following spring.

There are smaller-flowered hybrids in the 'Nanus' and 'Primulinus' groups and these flower in early summer. They are more suitable for mixed borders and if planted in a sheltered garden can survive when left in the ground all year.

▼ *Gladiolus* **'Princess Margaret Rose'**

Dahlias and begonias

Dahlias and begonias are often sold alongside summer bulbs but they are not reliably hardy and need lifting in autumn to protect them from freezing. They grow from tubers. Dahlias have elongated tubers clustered around the growing point, whereas begonias have a rounded tuber with a depression in the top from where the shoots erupt.

Dahlias can be grown in a mixed border, their bright colours provide some razzmatazz in late summer. Many are double-flowered forms but the single-flowered types are deservedly popular, especially 'Bishop of Llandaff', with its scarlet flowers and dark bronze foliage. Lift the tubers after the stems have been frosted for the first time and store them somewhere cool and dark for the winter.

Garden begonias are really meant for summer bedding, where their dazzling colours are put to good use. They are often sold by colour so take your pick and plant them just below soil level after the last frost, usually in early June.

▼ *Dahlia* **'Bishop of Llandaff'**

▲ *Dahlia* **'David Howard' in a mixed border**

▼ **Double red begonia**

Autumn

Colchicum

The flowers of colchicums first show at the tail end of summer. As the nights become colder and the days shorter, these pink goblets emerge from the soil where before there was nothing. Bejewelled with droplets of dew, the flowers open up with the first rays of sunlight on an autumn morning. One of their many common names is naked ladies, referring to the flowers that appear and fade before any sign of leaves. In a border, under shrubs or in grass at the foot of a tree, the naked colchicum flowers breathe new life into the garden just as summer's bounty is waning.

Another name for colchicums is autumn crocus but this is misleading. They are not crocus, and to add to the confusion, there are autumn-flowering species of true crocus. Colchicum flowers are generally larger than those of the crocus and the largest belong to *Colchicum speciosum*. The broad cups of this Turkish species are pink with a white throat. The throat narrows to a greenish floral tube that holds the open petals more than 20 cm above the soil from which the bud emerged. There is also a glorious pure white form, called 'Album'.

Colchicum autumnale is native to Europe, including Britain. Its pure pink blooms with a pale floral tube reach 15 cm tall and up to six can arise from one corm. It is sometimes called meadow saffron, which causes more confusion with crocus, as the true saffron crocus is *Crocus sativus*. *Colchicum autumnale* is one of the first colchicums to flower in the autumn garden and there is a white form, again called 'Album'. Other species, like *C. agrippinum* and to a lesser extent *C. cilicicum*, have delicate tessellations on their flowers, reminiscent of the snake's head fritillary but much paler.

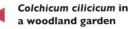

Colchicum cilicicum in a woodland garden

 Colchicum autumnale

Various other species are occasionally available, some very small, such as the dwarf pale pink C. *cupani*, and a few flower in spring, including the yellow C. *lutea*, but the overriding colour in the autumn plants is a shade of pink or pale violet. There are also various hybrids and the most distinctive of these is the double-flowered C. 'Waterlily'. This has a bunch of narrow petals that look remarkably like a floppy waterlily.

 Colchicum speciosum 'Album'

 Colchicum 'Waterlily'

 Colchicum speciosum

Planting colchicums

Most species of *Colchicum* are from the Mediterranean region, especially south-east Europe and Turkey. They are named after the ancient kingdom of Colchis, which was at the eastern end of the Black Sea. Many of them are adapted to a typical Mediterranean climate and flower as soon as the first rains of autumn have fallen after a long dry summer, but as you approach ancient Colchis along the northern coast of Turkey, the rainfall increases and can fall at any time of year. This makes some colchicums, like C. *speciosum*, well-adapted to wetter climates and they can be planted in a range of garden situations, as long as they get enough sunlight.

In a sunny border or under deciduous trees and shrubs, colchicums should thrive in any reasonably-drained soil. Plant the corms in summer, preferably before they flower, at a depth of 7–10 cm and even deeper for the largest. When planting, it is important to remember that when the flowers have gone the leaves will eventually appear and they are not always easy to accommodate in a border. The upsurge of wide, shiny leaves often covers a far greater area than the flowers ever did and they will last through to late spring. This is not such a problem with the smaller species, but for the largest you will have to be careful what you plant around them. Small spring bulbs cannot push through the colchicum leaves and once these leaves have died down you will be left with a gap in the border. This can be filled with later summer perennials, such as hostas or sprawling geraniums such as *Geranium* 'Ann Folkard'. If you plant colchicums in grass, you must delay mowing until early summer.

Autumn-flowering crocus

Best known for flowering in late winter and early spring, the genus *Crocus* includes a significant number of autumn-flowering species. Like winter-flowering crocus, they are summer dormant but they flower at the beginning of their growing season rather than at the end. Like colchicums, autumn-flowering crocus often flower before their foliage appears but the leaves soon elongate as soon as the flower begins to fade. The leaves are long but very narrow so do not have a huge impact on a border and are almost invisible in grass. The first blooms can appear in late summer, at the end of August, but the main flowering season is late September to early November. Plant the corms in summer, about 7–10 cm deep.

One of the best species for growing in grass is *Crocus speciosus*. Reaching 12–18 cm tall, the violet purple flowers are delicately patterned with darker veins. In the centre of the flower are three yellow anthers and a long, intricately divided, pale orange style. This species is ideal for a meadow where a few precocious blooms might appear just after the grass is cut down in August, but the main flowering period is September and October. They also look good at the base of a tree, where the grass is naturally thin because of the dry soil in summer, the perfect conditions for *Crocus*. In a border, choose a position with good drainage in full sun or the dappled shade of summer-flowering shrubs. The white form, *C. speciosus* 'Albus', has pure white petals with a touch of yellow in the throat and the same pale orange style. It looks particularly effective growing through dark foliage, such as that of *Ophiopogon planiscapus* 'Nigricans', the ghostly flowers emerging through the narrow black leaves.

▶ *Crocus speciosus* flowering in a meadow

▶ *Crocus speciosus* 'Albus' growing through the black leaves of *Ophiopogon planiscapus* 'Nigricans'

Crocus pulchellus

Crocus nudiflorus comes from the Pyrenees and the name refers to the flowers being 'nude' without their leaves. In this species, the flowers are a clean mauve-purple, with orange anthers and a pale yellow divided style. They appear in October, well before the foliage. The petals narrow to a long, thin floral tube that holds the bowl-shaped bloom 10–18 cm high. Well-drained soil and full sun suit this species, although a little shade will do no harm.

Other species to look out for include the pale blue-violet blooms of *C. pulchellus* and the lilac satin goblets of *C. goulimyi*. They have more rounded petals than *C. speciosus* and are shorter plants, growing between 10 and 15 cm tall. Both are from the sunny climes of south-east Europe and they are often seen in alpine house collections, lovingly cared for in pots of gritty soil and protected from rain. They can be grown equally well outside if the soil is very well-drained and they have plenty of sun.

Crocus goulimyi

Crocus nudiflorus

The saffron crocus

Saffron is harvested from the flowers of the autumn-flowering *Crocus sativus*. Used to flavour sauces and rice, saffron is the long, branched, orange-crimson style that dangles from the centre of the flower. Many flowers are needed to gather just a gram of saffron, making it the most expensive spice in the world by weight. Still cultivated in huge numbers in countries such as Iran and Morocco, saffron crocus was grown in the past as a crop in Britain, especially in East Anglia, around the town of Saffron Walden. It needs good drainage and, if it is to flower well, a sunny position in the garden. The flowers appear along with the leaves and remain open whatever the weather.

Crocus sativus

53

Autumn-flowering *Cyclamen*

There are few bulbs, corms or tuberous plants that are valued as much for their foliage as for their flowers, but cyclamen is one of them and this is especially true of *Cyclamen hederifolium*, the ivy-leaved cyclamen. This is one of the earliest autumn flowers, sometimes appearing in late July but it doesn't really get going until late August and September. The flowers come in shades of white to violet-pink and emerge before the leaves, on stems 10–12 cm tall. Then the triangular leaves unfold to reveal a complex kaleidoscope pattern of greens, cream and silvery grey. These leaves last through winter and into spring, forming a patchwork ground cover over otherwise bare soil. This is also one of the toughest cyclamen, fully hardy and tolerant of a range of garden conditions.

▼ **Cyclamen graecum**

All cyclamen grow from a rounded tuber. The roots grow from the base or around the sides and at the top of the tuber are small growing points from which the leaves and flowers appear. The tubers range from just a few centimetres across to ancient, knarled specimens of *C. hederifolium* that can be the size of a plate. Several flowers grow from one tuber and, in older plants, there may be a number of growing points that each give rise to a cluster of flowers. Each flower has its own stem, which is hooked over at the tip so that the flower points downwards, with the petals swept back and often twisted through 90 degrees, like the blades of a propeller. Flower colour is commonly pink but ranges from very pale pink to magenta, often with a darker blotch, smudge or streak at the mouth where the petal bends back. As the flower fades, the seed pod expands and at the same time the stem begins to coil like a spring, bringing the seed pod back down to earth. By summer, the seed pods have split open to release the fat, sticky seeds, beloved by ants that will carry them away, helping to distribute plants through the garden.

▼ **The patterned leaves of *Cyclamen hederifolium***

▲ *Cyclamen hederifolium*, the ivy-leaved cyclamen

Cyclamen hederifolium is the most commonly grown species and, along with winter-flowering *C. coum*, the most hardy and resilient cyclamen. These two species are the best for most gardens but if you want something a little different, there are other cyclamen to try. *Cyclamen cilicium* has dainty white or pale pink flowers above round, patterned leaves. This Turkish species needs a well-drained site in sun or partial shade. The flowers are held just 5–7 cm above the ground. Very similar is another Turkish species, *C. mirabile*, which has leaves that are often tinted with pink as they emerge.

For milder, sheltered gardens there are a few less hardy but very attractive autumn species. *Cyclamen graecum* has leaves that rival those of *C. hederifolium* for the variety of patterning they display. It has stocky flowers in rich, candy pink, as well as in white. It is also unique among cyclamen in having permanent fleshy roots attached to the base of the tuber, an important point to consider if you are growing this plant in a pot; the pot will have to be deep enough to accommodate those roots. Although not totally hardy, *C. graecum* does survive temperatures a few degrees below freezing if planted in a warm, sunny position and free-draining soil. The same is true for *C. africanum*, a species more at home in the warm Mediterranean climate found along the coasts of Algeria and Tunisia. This has some of the largest leaves in the genus, up to 15 cm across, and the flowers are very like those of *C. hederifolium* but held upright on stems 15–20 cm tall. Last in this select group is *C. cyprium*. Although this species is relatively hardy, its flowers appear in late autumn, in October and November, and can be damaged by harsh weather. These flowers are white with a magenta smudge on the base of each petal. It grows wild only on the island of Cyprus but can make a pretty plant for a sheltered spot in the garden or for growing in a pot.

Cyclamen africanum growing on the Rock Garden at Kew

▲ **Late-autumn flowers of *Cyclamen cyprium***

Buying and planting *Cyclamen*

Cyclamen tubers can be bought in summer when they are dormant but, as with bulbs like snowdrops and erythroniums, they do not like being dried out for too long, so get them early. Also, if bought when dormant, you cannot tell what shade of pink the flowers are, nor how the leaves are patterned. For these reason, it is usually best to buy cyclamen as growing plants in autumn or winter. Then you know exactly what you are getting and they are more likely to survive once planted in the garden.

Plant the tubers just below ground, with just 2 or 3 centimetres of soil over them. Well-drained, friable soil is ideal, and they can be located beneath shrubs in a border, among the roots at the base of a tree or in a raised bed or rock garden. *Cyclamen hederifolium*, sometimes sold under the old name of *C. neapolitanum*, can be grown in dappled shade — a woodland garden makes the perfect place to enjoy these autumn blooms but avoid deep shade and wet, heavy soil.

Cyclamen do not produce offsets. It is possible to propagate them by cutting up the tubers so that there is a growing point on each piece, but the most reliable way to increase your stock is to grow from seed. Left to their own devices in the garden, cyclamen will naturally spread but you can also collect seed and grow them yourself. You can then plant them where you want them, not where the ants think they should be, although this does sometimes lead to some pleasant surprises, as the flowers can appear unexpectedly in unusual places.

Sternbergia

Shades of pink, lilac, violet and purple dominate the colours of many autumn bulbs, so to make a change, consider planting some bulbs of *Sternbergia*. These produce goblets of bright, golden yellow. The flowers appear first, but the narrow, dark green leaves soon grow up alongside them, and the blooms open wide when the sun shines. The individual flowers are each held on their own green stem, like short daffodils (which are in the same family), and don't have the long floral tubes found in crocus and colchicums.

The main species of *Sternbergia* offered for sale is *S. lutea*. Wide flowers are held around 10–12 cm above ground in late September and October, and the leaves eventually grow taller. *Sternbergia sicula* is very similar but has smaller flowers and shorter leaves that don't usually extend beyond the flower. There are a few other species, including the white *S. candida* which flowers in early spring, but these rarities are for the bulb collector and in the garden the only one worth planting for display is the gorgeous *S. lutea*.

Sternbergias are bulbs from the Mediterranean region and western Asia, so they like a warm, dry summer. Plant them at the foot of a south- or west-facing wall or in a sunny border. Too much shade and they might not flower, and in wet, heavy soil they can easily rot away. They also don't mind being congested and can flower better when the bulbs are packed together. Don't try and rush nature, this clumping up will happen naturally as the bulbs grow and produce offsets. When you plant the bulbs, you still need to leave some space between each one, the sternbergias will do the rest.

Sternbergia lutea ▶

Nerines

One of the joys of autumn bulbs is their flowers, which seem to appear almost overnight without warning. Of all these autumnal surprises, none is more flamboyant than the striking nerines. Fat shoots push through surrounding plants, the flowers emerging from a pointed sheath that splits open to reveal the individual blooms, which are arranged at the top of the tall green stem. Each flower is a flared trumpet, split to its base. The petals surround dangling anthers on the ends of long, wiry filaments.

Nerines are South African bulbs and the most colourful is *Nerine sarniensis*, also known as the Guernsey lily. Unfortunately, this species is not hardy and if you want to enjoy the flowers, which come in shades of orange, red, white and pink, you will have to grow it in a container, kept frost free. Luckily there are some hardy members of this genus and the one that is likely to do best in most gardens is *N. bowdenii*.

The typical flower colour in *N. bowdenii* is bright pink but there are various cultivars with flowers of white to deep pink and magenta. Look out for pure white 'Alba' and the magenta-pink 'Isabel'. The flowers are held horizontally and face in all directions. There can be ten or more flowers at the top of the stem, which reaches up to 60 cm tall. The strap-like leaves appear later and last through spring and summer, leaving only a small window in early spring, between flowering and leaf growth, to plant the dormant bulbs. A sunny position with well-drained soil is best, such as in a gravel garden or the foot of a south-facing wall, where the warmth of the sun is captured. Plant the flask-shaped bulbs so that the tips are just at the soil surface. The hybrid *Nerine* 'Zeal Giant' is from a cross between *N. bowdenii* and *N. sarniensis* and has particularly large flowers of deep cerise pink.

▲ **Nerine bowdenii 'Alba'**

◀ **Nerine bowdenii 'Isabel'**

Nerine bowdenii in a gravel garden ▶

There are several other species of *Nerine*. Few are likely to be encountered outside of specialist collections but there are a couple to look out for. *Nerine undulata* needs a sunny, sheltered spot in the garden, with well-drained soil, where it will bloom in October and November on stems 40–50 cm tall. The flowers are mid-pink and the petals have wavy edges. Although it doesn't have flowers as large as those of *N. bowdenii*, *N. undulata* creates dense clumps over time that produce a profusion of flowering stems. *Nerine filifolia* is even shorter, growing to around 30 cm, and the flowers are especially spidery, with narrow, wavy-edged pink petals.

▼ **Nerine undulata on a rock garden**

South African bulbs

Although the majority of bulbs planted in European and North American gardens are from the Northern Hemisphere, one of the most important regions for bulb diversity in nature is South Africa. On the western side of the country, particularly in the Western Cape, the climate is Mediterranean, with long, dry summers and cool, wet winters. On the eastern side, the opposite is true: the winters are dry and the summers wet. Amongst the hills and mountains on both sides of the country are bulbous plants that have adapted to a dry season, whenever it occurs.

Relatively few South African bulbs are widely known in gardens. Some of the more exotic are not reliably hardy and so will never make good garden plants outside their native country, but there are some that have become well established in gardens. The deep blue flowers of *Agapanthus* are a familiar sight in milder areas, such as along the coast of south-west England. South African gladioli have been used to breed a range of colourful hybrids and in the same family is *Crocosmia*, also known as montbretia. These are able to survive in colder parts of the country, growing in the summer and dying back to fat corms in autumn. There are many crocosmia cultivars with flowers in colours ranging from yellow to scarlet and deep red. The leaves themselves are attractive; long, ridged swords shooting out of a sunny border. Closely related are the angel's fishing rods, *Dierama* and the exotic-looking *Ixia*. More and more bulbs from this country are being trialled in the open garden, so keep looking out for surprises; the world of bulbs still has a lot more to offer.

▼ **Crocosmia 'Spitfire'**   ▼ **Ixia maculata**

Glossary

Bulb
An underground storage organ made up of fleshy leaf bases surrounding a flattened stem. Most bulbs have layers of leaf bases with the oldest on the outside, usually enclosed in a brittle or papery tunic. Roots grow from the base.

Corm
An underground storage organ made from a swollen stem base. Corms are solid and usually renewed every year, with the new corm forming on top of the preceding one. Roots grow from the base.

Rhizome
An underground stem, often horizontal and creeping. Buds give rise to new leaves and roots. Often swollen to store nutrients.

Stolon
A stem that grows along the ground or below the surface. Sometimes called runners. They have buds that will form a new plant. Some bulbs produce stolons and in this way can spread without setting seed. Plants that do this are said to be stoloniferous.

Tuber
A swollen stem or root that works as an underground storage organ. Stem tubers, such as those of cyclamen, begonias and potatoes, have buds that give rise to new stems and roots. Root tubers, like dahlias, are modified roots and only form buds where they are attached to the stem.